Table of Contents

MyPlate

MyPlate is a tool that
helps you eat healthful food.
MyPlate reminds you
to limit the added sugars
and solid fats that you eat.

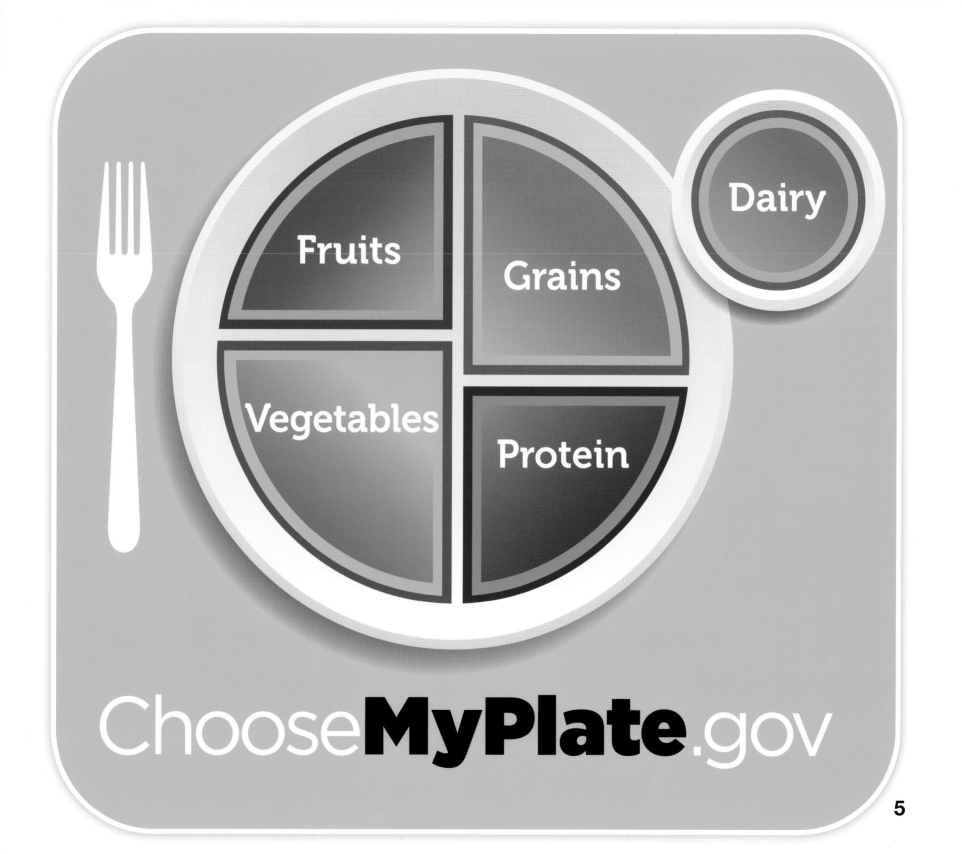

Fruits

Grains

Dairy

Vegetables

Protein

ChooseMyPlate.gov

Sugars and Fats

Sugar has very few nutrients. Some foods have natural sugars, such as fresh fruit. Avoid foods with added sugar.

7

Everyone needs to eat
some fat. It has nutrients.
But some fats are better
than others. Eat fewer foods
with solid fats, like french fries.

To grow healthy and strong,

limit your added sugars

and solid fats every day.

Eat sweets only as

a special treat.

Eat Smart

Enjoy sweets,

but eat fewer of them.

Share a small candy bar

with a friend.

When it's time for a snack,

skip the chips.

Enjoy fresh fruit instead.

After dinner choose
a healthy dessert.
Enjoy a baked apple
or a frozen juice bar.

Are you thirsty?

Sodas have added sugar.

Drink water, skim milk,

or a small glass of

100-percent juice instead.

Sweet Treats

Small amounts of sweets

make yummy treats

on special days.

Making Healthy Choices

Instead of this, eat this:

cheese puffs	string cheese
a hot dog	lean turkey slices
a candy bar	½ cup (60 mL) strawberries
chips	whole grain crackers
a donut	1 cup (120 mL) low fat yogurt
french fries	popcorn

Glossary

added sugar—any kind of sugar added to a food

MyPlate—a food plan that reminds people to eat healthful food and be active; MyPlate was created by the U.S. Department of Agriculture

nutrient—something that people need to eat to stay healthy and strong; vitamins and minerals are nutrients

snack—a small amount of food people eat between meals

solid fat—a kind of fat that is solid at room temperature; solid fat is also called saturated fat

sugar—a sweet substance that comes from plants

Read More

Olson, Gillia M. *MyPlate and You.* Health and Your Body. Mankato, Minn.: Capstone Press, 2012.

Sullivan, Jaclyn. *What's in Your Soda?* What's in Your Fast Food. New York: PowerKids Press, 2012.

Tieck, Sarah. *Eat Well.* Get Healthy. Minneapolis: ABDO Pub. Co., 2012.

Internet Sites

FactHound offers a safe, fun way to find Internet sites related to this book. All of the sites on FactHound have been researched by our staff.

Here's all you do:

Visit *www.facthound.com*

Type in this code: 9781429687461

 Check out projects, games and lots more at
www.capstonekids.com

Index

Word Count: 161
Grade: 1
Early-Intervention Level: 15